Understanding the Story of the Bible

An Introduction to Salvation History

by
Eileen Clare Grant

*All booklets are published thanks to the
generous support of the members of the
Catholic Truth Society*

CATHOLIC TRUTH SOCIETY
PUBLISHERS TO THE HOLY SEE

Contents

All rights reserved. First published 2013 by The Incorporated Catholic Truth Society, 40-46 Harleyford Road London SE11 5AY Tel: 020 7640 0042 Fax: 020 7640 0046. © The Incorporated Catholic Truth Society 2013.

ISBN 978 1 86082 845 4

Introduction

God loved the world so much that he gave his only Son, so that everyone who believes in him may not be lost but may have eternal life. For God sent his Son into the world not to condemn the world, but so that through him the world might be saved (*Jn* 3:16-17).

These words herald the beginning of the final part of the long story we call the History of Salvation. The *Catechism* tells us: "Creation is the foundation of 'all God's saving plans', the 'beginning of the history of salvation' (GCD 51) that culminates in Christ. Conversely, the mystery of Christ casts conclusive light on the mystery of creation and reveals the end for which 'in the beginning God created the heavens and the earth': from the beginning, God envisaged the glory of the new creation in Christ" (*Catechism of the Catholic Church* [henceforward *CCC*] par. 280.). Even before he created the world, God foresaw the unfolding of his eternal plan for the children he created out of love.

The Second Vatican Council recounted how "God, who through the Word creates all things and keeps them in existence, gives men an enduring witness to Himself in created realities. Planning to make known the way of heavenly salvation, He went further and from the start manifested Himself to our first parents. Then, after their fall His promise of redemption aroused in them the hope of being saved and from that time on He ceaselessly kept the human race in His care, to give eternal life to those who perseveringly do good in search of salvation" (*Dei Verbum* c.3.).

After their fall from grace, God did not leave our first parents alone and desolate in a world suddenly become harsh and alien to them; he clothed their nakedness and continued to give them signs of his love for them and his compassion for their plight. God is a Father as no human father can be father and he knew not to overburden his immature and wayward children with too much knowledge at any one time. Instead, like a loving and patient teacher, he gradually unfolded his revelation, his plan for the ultimate salvation of those children. He did this over many centuries, through many different scribes and prophets, in many different forms, in the narrative we now know as the Old Testament, the Book of the Old Covenant. With what Hans Urs von Balthasar called "the long patience of God", in his yearning for his children to return to him with purified hearts, God did not hasten the unfolding of his plan but provided time and opportunity in which to repent and undergo a true conversion, a turning back towards the destiny prepared for us before the foundation of the world.

For the earliest revelation of his salvific plan, God chose one small people, the Jews, to be his own special family and through them he proceeded to put this plan into action, gradually instructing them through chosen individuals and ensuing events. God made a Covenant with those in human history we know as the Patriarchs: first with Noah, after another fall from grace by humankind, then definitively with Abraham, a man of obedience and trust, the father of countless generations. This was ratified on Mount Sinai with Moses, God's chosen instrument to lead his people out of slavery and into the Promised Land, and to whom he gave his Law. Finally he promised to King David, a "son of Abraham", the founding of an everlasting kingdom. During these ancient times, he called many other men and women to manifest his deeds and his glory. Through his chosen prophets, God called his people to repentance and foretold a future salvation through a new and everlasting Covenant and a *Messiah*, a *Christ*, God's Anointed One, who would come to save all men from sin and death and usher in a new and eternal Paradise.

When St Matthew, a Jew, placed at the very beginning of his Gospel a genealogy, a "family tree" of Jesus, he named him as "son of David, son of Abraham" (1:1). Recounting the Good News of salvation through

Christ for Jewish converts to the new "way", Matthew was at pains to stress Jesus's Jewish credentials and his definitive role as the culmination of all God's promises through the Patriarchs and Prophets. St Luke went even further, tracing the lineage of Jesus right back to Adam, "son of God" (3:38).

> See, the days are coming - it is the LORD who speaks - when I will make a new Covenant with the House of Israel (and the House of Judah) (*Jr* 31:31).

The New Testament authors saw this text from the prophet Jeremiah as pointing towards the New Covenant definitively realised in Jesus Christ, God-with-us, God made flesh, God come amongst sinful humanity, when what was once offered to one people, the Jews, would be extended also to the Gentiles, to all the nations of the earth.

Salvation History is, simply, the whole story of humankind and the world in which we live, from the moment of the first recorded sin of our first parents to the *parousia*, the Second Coming of Jesus Christ at the end of time when all will be finally gathered up and offered back to the Father, a consummation for which we pray in every Mass, "as we await the blessed hope, and the coming of our Saviour, Jesus Christ". It is, therefore, the true history of the world, the recounting of which is a gift from God to enable us to understand our human condition and to strive with his help to rise up out of the darkness into which we have fallen.

He has let us know the mystery of his purpose, the hidden plan he so kindly made in Christ from the beginning, to act upon when the times had run their course to the end: that he would bring everything together under Christ, as head, everything in the heavens and everything on earth (*Ep* 1:9-10).

In the Beginning…

Salvation became necessary when the first human beings fell from the state of grace in which God had created them. Of all the creatures God had made, man alone was formed in God's own image and likeness and set above all the other things he had created. These other creatures were of flesh only; the angels, God's servants in heaven, were of spirit only; only human beings were created as both flesh and spirit, rational beings who would tend God's created world in the day and, in the evening, "in the cool of the day", would walk and talk with their heavenly Father.

All that God made he gave as an unmerited gift to his children, simply because he loved them. All he asked in return was that they should trust him and obey the one condition he asked of them - something they, in their turn, could offer back to him. Sadly, as we know, they failed in trust, disobeyed and realised the appalling consequences when it was too late: through their transgression, first sin then death entered the world and human history. Yet God never failed in his love for his children and gave them a hint of hope in his "proto-evangelium", the "first gospel":

I will make you enemies of each other: you [the serpent] and the woman, your offspring and her offspring. It will crush your head and you will strike its heel (*Gn* 3:15).

The rest, as they say, is history - the history of salvation. What came to be called "salvation history" is gradually outlined throughout the Old Testament from the moment our first parents sadly departed from the "garden" in which they had been placed by God. The human writers of the Old Testament stories sometimes describe God as being angry with his people, but at other times they stress his unconditional love. These writers were called by God, commissioned by him to talk to his people, but they had to rely on their own human knowledge, human circumstances and human emotions and described God and his plan accordingly. But it is God's love that always wins through in the end.

"[Christ] for our sake paid Adam's debt to the eternal Father, and, pouring out his own dear Blood, wiped clean the record of our ancient sinfulness" (The *Exultet*).

When our first parents turned away from God, this had an effect on everything around them and on all future beings: the whole of creation fell with them. At first, human beings were said to have lived to a great old age;

the further and longer they were away from the garden, the shorter human life-spans became until, as the Psalmist said: "Our span is seventy years, or eighty for those who are strong" (*Ps* 89:10). And sin grew and spread.

Sin and death

Adam and Eve produced children; the best-known are their two first-born, Cain and Abel. Cain was a farmer and Abel a shepherd (later seen by the Church Fathers as a "type" of Christ). "Cain brought some of the produce of the soil as an offering for the LORD, while Abel for his part brought the first-born of his flock and some of their fat as well" (*Gn* 4:3-4). Abel found favour with the Lord because he gave of his best: as the writer of the Letter to the Hebrews was later to observe, "It was because of his faith that Abel offered God a better sacrifice than Cain, and for that he was declared to be righteous when God made acknowledgement of his offerings" (*Heb* 11:4). Cain, we are told, was "very angry" but the Lord bade him strive to master his inclination to sin (an inclination, "concupiscence", that has been passed down to all humanity). The American writer John Steinbeck became fascinated with this passage of Scripture and wove a lengthy novel - *East of Eden* - around the concept of human free will: that we have a choice between doing good or evil, of mastering the tendency to sin or of giving in to it. The novel is peopled with characters who are faced with these choices and it is only at the end of the story that finally one person takes responsibility for his actions which have led to the death of his twin brother.

> If you are well disposed, ought you not to lift up your head? But if you are ill disposed, is not sin at the door like a crouching beast hungering for you, which you must master? (*Gn* 4:7)

Cain ignored God's counsel and, in a jealous rage, he murdered his brother - the first recorded murder in history. Already, then, we see how sin spreads and how it damages relationship even further. God did not destroy Cain for his crime but sent him away, to a land "east of Eden", to be a perpetual wanderer. Six generations later, we learn, three brothers amongst his descendants - Jabal the nomadic shepherd, Jubal the forefather of itinerant musicians and Tubal Cain, the first blacksmith (once an itinerant trade) - were continuing to live out Cain's restless destiny.

Adam and Eve had a third son, named Seth, and a descendant of his was Enoch, great-grandfather of Noah. Enoch won God's favour and, Scripture tells us, did not die like the others: "Enoch walked with God. Then he vanished because God took him" (*Gn* 5:24); and Sirach also says: "Enoch pleased the Lord, and was taken up, an example for the conversion of all generations" (*Si* 44:16).

God renews his creation

After this episode evil gradually spread throughout the world and eventually God decided to start again (*Gn* 6-9).

> Noah was found perfectly virtuous, in the time of wrath he became the scion: because of him a remnant was preserved for the earth at the coming of the Flood. Everlasting Covenants were made with him that never again should every living creature perish by flood (*Si* 44:17-18).

God did not, however, destroy absolutely everything that he had made. He chose Noah, a "righteous" man (six hundred years old at the time) who was given very detailed instructions for building an "ark", a huge vessel which would keep Noah, his wife, his three sons Ham, Shem and Japheth, and their wives, safe from the great flood that was to be sent upon the earth. Noah was told also to gather representatives of every species of creature and every kind of foodstuff and take these also into the ark. "Noah did this; he did all that God had ordered him" (*Gn* 6:22). Eventually the waters began to recede and Noah sent out first a raven which found no tree on which to alight, then a dove which returned with an olive branch in its beak; thus a dove bearing an olive branch has become a symbol of good news and, by extension, of peace. Noah and his family and all living creatures

with them were at last able to come out of the ark and
live on the land again. Many other ancient religions
record similar myths of a great flood as a consequence
of human wickedness.

On dry land Noah offered a sacrifice of thanksgiving to
the Lord. God blessed him, then established a Covenant
with Noah, his descendants and all living creatures, with
a rainbow as "a sign of the Covenant between me and the
earth", that "no thing of flesh shall be swept away again
by the waters of the flood". God promised that he would
"call to mind the lasting Covenant between God and
every living creature of every kind that is found on the
earth" (*Gn* 9:11-16). God's promise to Noah eventually
came to perfect fulfilment in Jesus Christ who promised
to remain with us always (*Mt* 28:20). It was also at this
time that God gave human beings permission to kill
animals for food, although "you must not eat flesh with
life, that is to say blood, in it" (*Gn* 9:4).

Pride and confusion

Again God instructed his chosen ones to "be fruitful,
multiply, and fill the earth", and gradually the earth
became more populous. At this time, we read,
"throughout the earth men spoke the same language,
with the same vocabulary" and so the people gathered
together and planned to build a great city in the form of

a tower reaching all the way to heaven, thus attempting once more to make themselves "as God". In response to their pride and presumption God scattered them and confused their language so that they could no longer understand one another and were unable to complete the tower (*Gn* 11). This tower then became known as "Babel", from a Hebrew word meaning "to confuse"; it features in many well-known paintings, including one by the artist Pieter Brueghel the Elder. The word has come into our language to suggest a meaningless babble of voices out of which nothing can be clearly distinguished. This "confusion" was reversed at Pentecost when the Holy Spirit came down upon the apostles; they were suddenly able to speak in all the different languages of visitors to Jerusalem, and all humanity was called to come together once more as one family in Christ.

Many generations later, a descendant of Noah's son Shem, by name Terah, lived and died in Ur, city of the Chaldeans, leaving behind him two sons, one of whom was named Abram, whose wife was named Sarai.

Abraham, our Father in Faith

God's plan

At a certain point in human history, God began to reveal to human beings something of his great redemptive plan for them: this we call *Divine Revelation*. God singled out certain tribes and told them that they would be his chosen people and he would be their God.

From amongst these tribes, he chose Abraham and promised that his descendants would be more numerous than the stars in the heavens or the grains of sand on the shore. When this "friend of God" first appeared on the scene, he was named Abram ("exalted father") and his wife was named Sarai. God told Abram to take his family and go to the land that God would point out to him. This was expecting a great deal of Abram: the journey would be long and hazardous, through the lands of possibly hostile tribes; all his household goods, tents, herds and servants had to be gathered together; and he had no idea where they were actually going or what they might find when they got there. Abram, however, despite natural fears, had trust in his God and he obeyed, departing with his household and that of his nephew Lot.

Eventually they arrived in Canaan, where Abram built near Bethel an altar to the Lord, who again appeared to him, promising him this land. To escape famine, Abram moved on into Egypt for a short time, but soon returned to Bethel. There was not enough land to support both his and Lot's households, leading to quarrels between their respective herdsmen, so they separated: Lot chose for himself the fertile Jordan valley and went to dwell in the city of Sodom, near the Dead Sea. Abram remained in Canaan where the Lord promised him all the land he could see to north, south, east and west. Abram settled in the hill country near Hebron, at a place known as the Oaks of Mamre. Later God made a solemn Covenant with Abram, binding on both sides, prophesying slavery in a strange land for his descendants, but also many lands and innumerable descendants.

When Lot and his family were captured by neighbouring kings, Abram came to their rescue. On his return to Canaan, he was greeted by the mysterious Melchizedek, king of Salem and "priest of God Most High". Melchizedek shared "bread and wine" with Abram, blessing him in the name of the Lord. This incident is seen as affirming the existence of the one true God and the significance of Israel in his plan; Melchizedek is seen also as a "type" of Christ and the sharing of bread and wine as a prefiguring of the Eucharist. The words "you are a priest for ever, a priest like Melchizedek of old" (*Ps* 109) are still used in the liturgy of priestly ordination.

God's promise to Abraham

A grief that Abram and Sarai shared was that they had no children, so eventually Sarai gave Hagar, her handmaid, to Abram that he might have a child by her. Such a practice was standard at the time and was even referred to in legal codes of the period. Hagar bore Abram a son whom he named Ishmael ("God hears"). Later, when Abram was an old man, God told him that from now on he was to be called Abraham, a sign of his new role in God's plan:

> Here now is my Covenant with you: you shall become the father of a multitude of nations. You shall no longer be called Abram; your name shall be Abraham, for I make you father of a multitude of nations. I will make you most fruitful. I will make you into nations, and your issue shall be kings. I will establish my Covenant between myself and you, and your descendants after you, generation after generation, a Covenant in perpetuity, to be your God and the God of your descendants after you (*Gn* 17:4-7).

God told him also that he would have a son by Sarai, now to be known as Sarah ("princess"). At the idea of having a son in their extreme old age, Abraham laughed.

When Sarah heard this news, she too laughed. The promise was solemnly made to them at Mamre by three men who suddenly appeared one day before them: "The Lord appeared to him at the Oak of Mamre while he was sitting by the entrance of the tent". This is one of the most mulled over passages in Scripture: the "men" are three - and they are one - and Abraham addresses them as "My Lord"; is it a first suggestion of the Holy Trinity? Christian painting and iconography have frequently interpreted the incident as such, most famously in the work of the Russian iconographer Andrei Rublev.

Before that longed-for son was born, God decided to destroy the city of Sodom, where Lot was living, because of the extreme wickedness of its people. Abraham pleaded with God that all should be spared if fifty just men could be found there; God agreed. But then Abraham worried about finding fifty and suggested instead forty-five, then forty, then thirty-five and so on, eventually reaching a mere ten. Each time, God agreed to be merciful. Persistence in prayer works! Unfortunately, there were no other righteous people in the city and only Lot and his family were saved. Lot's wife, however, came to an unfortunate end when she looked back at the destruction of the city and was turned into a pillar of salt. There are legends in other ancient civilisations of similar destruction and even archaeological evidence also points towards some momentous event in ancient history.

As God had promised, Sarah conceived in her old age and bore a son, naming him, as God had decreed, Isaac, which means "he laughs". For, as Sarah rejoiced: "God has given me cause to laugh." Unfortunately, however, Sarah was jealous of Hagar and her son Ishmael, and prevailed upon Abraham to banish them. He reluctantly agreed, trusting in God's promise that Ishmael too would prosper and become the father of a great nation. Ishmael did in fact become the ancestor of many Arabian tribes; Isaac's son Esau married a woman from one of them and Isaac's grandson Joseph was bought by Ishmaelite nomad merchants and sold into slavery in Egypt. God does indeed work in mysterious ways. Tradition has it that Ishmael is in fact the "father" of the Islamic peoples and they too see God as one who keeps his promises.

Abraham's faith in God

Abraham is called "our father in faith" because of his great trust in God and his promises. Having obeyed God in everything he had asked, he even set out to obey when God asked him to sacrifice his beloved son Isaac. Abraham loved his son - "your only son Isaac, whom you love" - and did not understand God's plan, but he trusted his God and knew that somehow everything would be well. Isaac too trusted his father and went willingly with him. As Christ was to do, Isaac carried on his back the wood for the sacrifice. This account was never meant as a tale of an unnaturally cruel father but as an illustration of supreme trust in God's promises, and has come to be seen as a prefiguring of Christ's willing self-sacrifice for us: "God himself will provide the lamb." It represents trust of the very highest order. When God saw Abraham's great faith he provided a ram for the sacrifice and repeated his promise to Abraham to make him the father of countless descendants. This passage of Scripture is read at the Paschal Vigil, in preparation for the great celebration of the Resurrection and invites catechumens and all the baptised to make their act of faith in the Lord.

> Because you have done this, because you have not refused me your son, your only son, I will shower blessings on you, I will make your descendants as many as the stars of heaven and the grains of sand on the seashore....All the nations of the earth shall bless themselves by your descendants, as a reward for your obedience (*Gn* 22:16-18).

Jacob and Joseph

God's faithfulness

Because God always keeps his promises, keeps his side of the Covenant, the boy Isaac grew up. In extreme old age, Abraham became anxious to find a suitable wife for his son, a wife not from the people among whom he now lived, but from his homeland far away. He therefore ordered his oldest servant to travel there and choose a wife for Isaac. The servant "set out for Aram Naharaiim and Nahor's town" (Nahor was Abraham's brother), laden with gifts for the prospective bride. There, by a spring of water, he met Rebekah, the daughter of Bethuel, "son of Milcah, wife of Abraham's brother Nahor". The servant praised God for leading him to the house of his master's kinsmen. Permission was granted for Rebekah to go to Canaan and marry Isaac. As she was approaching the lands of Abraham, she saw Isaac "walking in the fields as evening fell". Isaac looked at Rebekah; she looked at him; and they loved each other in that first moment. The fruit of their union was twins, two sons, Esau and Jacob, with the first-born, Esau, his father's heir. In traditional sibling rivalry, Jacob was jealous of his elder brother and, with his mother's help, cheated him of his birthright, securing by trickery his nearly blind father's blessing - a blessing which signified being identified as the father's heir (*Gn* 27). Then, being afraid of his brother's righteous anger, he fled from his home and found work with his uncle, Laban, in Chaldea. Along the way he had a dream in which he saw angels going up and down a ladder reaching up to heaven. In the dream God promised to him and his descendants the land on which he was lying.

In Chaldea, Jacob met and fell in love with Laban's younger daughter, Rachel, and asked for her as his wife. Laban agreed but ordered Jacob to give him seven years' labour before the marriage could take place. When the seven years were up, he then tricked Jacob into marrying the elder daughter, Leah, first. In those days, a form of polygamy was permitted, so after working for Laban for another seven years, Jacob was finally allowed to marry Rachel (*Gn* 29). Leah bore him five sons while Rachel remained barren; this made her so unhappy that she sent her maid to Jacob to bear a child by proxy. Leah also did this: it was a practice widely employed at the time. Then Leah had another two sons and a daughter, Dinah. Eventually, Rachel gave birth to a son, Joseph; much later she had another son named Benjamin. Rachel's weeping for her longed-for children came to personify women's lamentation over lost children and echoes down through the ages to the coming of Jesus in the flesh and the "slaughter of the innocents":

A voice was heard in Ramah,
sobbing and loudly lamenting:
it was Rachel weeping for her children,
refusing to be comforted
because they were no more
(*Mt* 2:18; cf *Jr* 31:15)

These stories also exemplify God's faithfulness to man, even when man is devious and untrusting, and how God's plan is not frustrated by human unreliability and double dealing.

Jacob's sons

Between his two wives, twelve sons were born for Jacob: Reuben, Simeon, Levi, Judah, Dan, Naphtali, Gad, Asher, Isachar, Zebulun, Joseph and Benjamin. Apart from Levi and Joseph, their names were to be given to the tribes of Israel, each with its own territory; Levi's tribe was set aside to serve as priests. The sons of Joseph - Ephraim and Manasseh - with their households were also given the status of independent tribes with their own territory. Jacob, like so many of God's chosen ones, and like many of the individuals in the genealogy of Jesus recounted in the Gospels of Matthew and Luke, is an inspiring example of how God does not see as men see but often chooses the seemingly weak and unworthy. Likewise, many times throughout the history of the chosen people, it is a younger son who wins God's favour and help.

After Joseph's birth, Jacob asked Laban to give him his wages and to let him take his family home so that he could make his peace with Isaac and Esau. Laban was reluctant for them to go and made things as difficult as he could for Jacob. Eventually, however, after various problems and solutions and stratagems, Jacob was allowed to leave peacefully, taking with him all his family and all the "striped or spotted or piebald" sheep from Laban's flocks: hence what we now call "Jacob sheep" (*Gn* 31). It was a special coat made from the wool of these sheep that Jacob was later to give Joseph as a sign of his favour. On the journey back to Canaan, Jacob had a strange encounter with a man who wrestled with him until dawn. Jacob realised that this man was an angel from God and asked for his blessing. The angel blessed him, saying: "Your name shall no longer be Jacob, but Israel [meaning *He who strives with God* or *God strives*], because you have been strong against God, you shall prevail against men" (*Gn* 32:29). Despite his understandable fear at the prospect of meeting Esau again, Jacob was welcomed back by his elder brother and they both wept with joy. Jacob reached his father's home at Mamre in time to see Isaac before he died and the reconciled brothers buried their father together. Centuries later, those who listen to Jesus telling the parable of the Prodigal Son would have been familiar with this story of reconciliation.

Joseph and his brothers - God brings good from evil

Joseph was the apple of Jacob's eye, being child of his beloved Rachel, and his father lavished gifts upon him. Joseph was also an interpreter of dreams, leading to further favours, including his famous distinctive coat. This is usually called the "coat of many colours", although it was probably not actually technicoloured, but woven in shades of grey and brown; some translations call it "a coat with long sleeves". He thus incurred the jealousy of his brothers who plotted together to get rid of him. At first they planned to kill him but instead cast him into a deep well, then sold him into slavery to a caravan of Ishmaelite merchants on their way to Egypt. The brothers took Joseph's coat, covered with blood, home to their father, telling him that Joseph had been devoured by wild beasts. Jacob mourned for his favourite child, saying he would weep for him until death (*Gn* 37).

In Egypt, Joseph was sold to Potiphar, chief of Pharaoh's guards. Unfortunately, Potiphar's wife took a fancy to young Joseph who, being loyal to his master and faithful to his God, rejected her advances. Annoyed at this, she accused him of trying to seduce her and he was thrown into prison. There he soon endeared himself to his fellow inmates, and to the warden, earning a reputation as an interpreter of dreams. Hearing eventually of Joseph's skill, Pharaoh sent for him and asked him to interpret the strange, troubling dreams he had been having. Joseph did so, warning him of a great famine to come - "Seven years are coming, bringing great plenty to the whole land of Egypt, but seven years of famine will follow them" - thus giving Pharaoh time to prepare for hard times (*Gn* 39-41).

As a reward, Joseph was raised to high office in Egypt. The famine extended throughout that whole part of the world, including the land where Jacob and his family were living, and Jacob sent his older sons to buy grain in Egypt. Joseph recognised them, though they did not know him. Joseph pretended to distrust them, accusing them of being spies, then, holding Simeon as hostage, sent the others back to Canaan, ordering them to return with their youngest brother Benjamin, born since Joseph's enslavement, as proof of their good faith. Joseph gave orders to fill their sacks with grain and secretly to return their money; when this was discovered by the brothers, they were afraid and saw the hand of God in it. At first Jacob refused to let Benjamin be taken from him, but he was eventually forced by the continuing famine to agree (*Gn* 42).

A second time the brothers went into Egypt to buy grain, this time taking gifts and their brother Benjamin with them. Joseph quickly came to love his youngest brother - "his heart was moved at the sight of his brother and he was near to weeping" (*Gn* 43:30) - and he did all he could to keep Benjamin in Egypt, even going to the extent of having a precious goblet hidden in his youngest brother's baggage and accusing him of theft. He found it impossible to keep up the pretence, however, and finally revealed his identity to his brothers. Any thoughts of vengeance were abandoned and, sending them home with many lavish gifts and provisions, he urged them to return with Jacob and all his household to settle in Egypt where they would be safe from all threat of famine. For Joseph's sake, Pharaoh was pleased to agree to this plan.

God spoke to Jacob (also known as "Israel") in a dream and repeated his promise to make a great nation of his people: "I myself will go down to Egypt with you. I myself will bring you back again, and Joseph's hand shall close your eyes" (*Gn* 46:2). Then Jacob and all his people travelled into Egypt where Jacob was reunited with Joseph amidst much tearful rejoicing. Pharaoh granted to the Hebrews the land of Goshen, in the eastern part of the Nile delta. Jacob survived for another seventeen years and, when close to death, he carried out two solemn blessings: firstly, on Joseph's two sons, Ephraim and Manasseh, recognising them as his own. The second blessing was of his own children and, along with the first blessing, marked the solemn institution of the twelve tribes of Israel.

The story of Joseph is a wonderful illustration of divine providence, of how God always works to bring good out of evil: "So it was not you who sent me here but God," Joseph said to his brothers when they are finally reconciled. "The evil you planned to do me has by God's design been turned to good, that he might bring about, as indeed he has, the deliverance of a numerous people" (*Gn* 45:8, 50:20), for, as St Paul reminds us, "we know that by turning everything to their good God co-operates with all those who love him, with all those that he has called according to his purpose" (*Rm* 8:28).

On his father's death, Joseph carried out Jacob's dying wish to be buried in the land where he was born. With Pharaoh's permission, Joseph and a huge company travelled into Canaan where he laid Jacob to rest in a tomb near Mamre - the place where Abraham had entertained the three "angels" and God had made his solemn promise to him. Joseph then returned into Egypt (*Gn* 43 and following).

Moses and the Exodus

God speaks to his people

The Hebrew people remained there for many years; they prospered and multiplied, "so they filled the land", until one day there arose a new Pharaoh "who knew nothing of Joseph". Then things changed drastically for the Hebrew people. The new Pharaoh became uneasy about their great numbers and enslaved them. He also gave orders that every male baby born to them must be killed. A woman belonging to the priestly tribe of Levi gave birth to a baby boy whom she managed to keep hidden for three months. When he grew too big to hide, she put him in a basket which she placed in the reeds on the bank of the river Nile while his sister kept watch. Pharaoh's daughter discovered the baby and, taking pity on him, she decided to rear him as her own child. The baby's sister helpfully offered to find a nurse for him and fetched their own mother who continued to care for the child until he was old enough to leave her.

When Moses grew up, presumably having at some point become aware of his origins, one day he killed an Egyptian guard whom he saw beating a Hebrew slave; Moses then fled from Egypt to escape Pharaoh's vengeance. He went to Midian where he rendered aid to the local priest's daughters who were being prevented by shepherds from watering their flocks at a well. The priest, Jethro, made him welcome. Moses subsequently married one of the daughters, Zipporah, who bore him two sons, and he remained in Midian tending his father-in-law's sheep. One day, in the wilderness, at Mount Horeb (Sinai), "the mountain of the Lord", he suddenly came upon a burning bush: it was burning steadily but was not being consumed. God called to him from the midst of the bush and Moses realised that he was in the presence of the Divine. The Lord explained to him how he had seen his chosen people's distress and had resolved to save them from their captivity. He told Moses that he must lead the Hebrew people out of Egypt to the land that their God had chosen for them: a land "where milk and honey flow". Moses did not feel up to the task: he was afraid of Pharaoh's anger and afraid also that the people would not listen to him. How could he return to Egypt, risking his life, to announce that a burning bush had given him his instructions? God proceeded to demolish all Moses's objections. It was at this moment God came nearest to revealing his name; he told Moses: "I AM WHO I AM" (Hebrew YHWH), that is, God is defined, named, identified, by his very being. God gave

Moses other signs to convince the people. When Moses reminded God that he had a stammer, God responded that his brother Aaron could do the talking for him. Here, as so often, God chooses a messenger whose reluctance and apparent unsuitability are no obstacle to what God wants to do; in fact, they only go to point up God's power working through him.

The people did accept what Moses told them, but when he and Aaron went to Pharaoh, Pharaoh refused to let the Hebrews go. To persuade him, God sent upon the Egyptians a series of plagues, each one more terrible than the one before: the Nile and all the water in Egypt turned into blood; a plague of frogs; one of mosquitoes; another of gadflies; disease of livestock; boils; a storm of hail; swarms of locusts; darkness, "darkness so thick that it can be felt". Pharaoh's heart, however, grew harder and eventually God sent the last and most terrible plague which would claim the life of the eldest male in every family, both humans and livestock. He then gave Moses instructions for the coming night when death was to come upon the Egyptians, and when the Israelites must make ready to leave Egypt. This is the origin of the Jewish Passover feast and God gave very precise instructions about the preparations for it, commanding that this day would forever afterwards be a day of festival for the people of Israel. They were to prepare lambs to be roasted whole, with unleavened bread and bitter herbs.

Blood from the slaughtered lambs was to be smeared on the doorposts of their homes so that the Lord's angel of death, passing over, would know which were the Hebrew houses. This event is seen as a prefiguring of the institution of the Eucharist and is recounted at the Mass of the Lord's Supper on Maundy Thursday.

God rescues his people

Everything happened as God had said and the Israelites were allowed to leave that night. The Lord travelled with them as a pillar of cloud in the day and a pillar of fire at night. Pharaoh, however, changed his mind and pursued the Israelites with a vast army until they came to the banks of the Red Sea. With God's help Moses made the sea part so that he and his people were able to pass through to the other side. When the Egyptians tried to follow, the sea fell back upon them and they were all drowned. This crossing of the Red Sea came to be seen as a "type" of baptism and must always be read at the Paschal Vigil, which is the archetypal time for baptisms. In baptism we die to sin and rise again with Christ to new life. In the waters of the Red Sea we see a type, or pattern, of our triumphant delivery from the slavery of sin just as the Israelites experienced their deliverance from physical slavery in Egypt. When we hear of the doomed Egyptians' watery death, we are reminded of the symbolic washing away of sin. The waters represent salvation to God's faithful children and destruction to the powers of evil.

> Baptism is not modelled after the crossing of the Red Sea; but neither is the account of the crossing simply an illustrated explanation of the baptismal rite. Instead, baptism is a continuation of the account of the crossing. The passage through the sea takes place this night...it will be ever more real as we approach closer and closer to the promised land. (Adrien Nocent, *The Liturgical Year* Vol. 3, Liturgical Press, 1977)

The passage of the Red Sea can also be seen as an image of God's victory over the death that surrounds us before and behind, and seems unavoidable. By God's power we enter into the waters of death and pass though them to life renewed.

God accompanies his people

Afterwards the Israelites wandered through the wilderness for forty years, having various adventures, overcoming enemies they encountered, gradually growing tired of wandering and blaming Moses for taking them away from what now seemed a more comfortable life in slavery. Many of their complaints were that they were hungry and thirsty: God sent quails and "manna" (meaning perhaps "what is it?") from heaven for them to eat. On another occasion he enabled Moses to bring a spring of water from a rock for the people to drink.

When they reached Mount Sinai, Moses went up the mountain to confer with God and God gave him his Law, his "Ten Words" or Commandments, along with other instructions as to their future behaviour. Moses passed all this on to the people and on a later trip up the mountain he received from God the Ten Commandments written on two tablets of stone. God gave Moses detailed plans for constructing an "ark", a small portable box, in which they were to carry the tablets throughout the rest of their journey, and for making a "tabernacle", a special decorated tent in which to place the ark. Moses spent so long on the mountaintop this time that the people grew bored and restless and had a golden calf made for their worship, similar to the pagan idols they had encountered on their travels.

Moses was so furious with them when he saw this that he smashed the tablets of stone. When he became calmer he interceded with the Lord who agreed not to punish the people as they deserved. Like Abraham before him, Moses is a wonderful example of intercessory prayer. God rewrote the Commandments on another two tablets of stone and the "Ark of the Covenant" was constructed according to his instructions. When Moses returned after speaking with God this time, his face shone so brightly with reflected glory that the people could not look upon it and he had to cover his face.

After many other experiences, and the drawing up of what became known as the Mosaic Law - hundreds of precepts regarding all manner of things - Canaan, the Promised Land, was eventually reached after forty years of wandering. Moses died before they entered there, because of a fault on his part, and his lieutenant and successor Joshua led the people across the Jordan. Moses has no recorded burial place, however, and in Christ's time, when he appears with Jesus to Peter, James and John on the mountaintop at the Transfiguration, there is a suggestion he was in fact taken straight up into heaven. This incident is believed to have taken place during the Feast of Tabernacles, a time when the Jews looked back to the time when God lived or "tabernacled" with them when they wandered for forty years in the wilderness; they looked forward also to the time when he would return and live with them again. Christians have the joy of knowing that the Lord has in fact come to live amongst his people - in "The Word was made flesh, he lived among us", the Greek word used by St John for "lived" means "tabernacled, pitched his tent". Our ancestors in faith remind themselves each year at the Passover how God is always with them in their travails just as every year we remember Christ's saving sacrifice on the cross.

The Heroes and the Judges: Deborah, Gideon and Samson

God calls his people back

After the triumphant entry into the Promised Land, the Israelites settled into Canaan and the Twelve Tribes were given their own territories. After Joshua's death, the people lapsed into idol worship and there were rebellions and defeats at the hands of their enemies. These difficult times were sometimes relieved by being ruled by a succession of heroes, also known as "judges", amongst whom were Samson, Gideon and Deborah.

Deborah was a prophetess who lived in the hill country of Ephraim, between Ramah and Bethel. When Israel had been subjugated by the Canaanites and had been oppressed for many years, she, in the name of the Lord God of Israel, called upon Barak, one of the judges from Naphtali, to gather an army to free their people. Barak agreed, on condition that Deborah accompany him; she agreed but warned him that it would not lead to his glory "for the Lord will deliver Sisera into the hands of a woman". Barak comprehensively defeated the Canaanite army but their commander Sisera escaped. Under pretence of offering him sanctuary, Jael, wife of a nomadic king who had secretly switched sides, killed him by driving a tent peg through his temple, "right through to the ground". Thus Deborah's prophecy came true (Jg 4:9; 4:21).

Gideon (the name means "warrior") was a young man belonging to the tribe of Manasseh. When the Israelites were suffering from attacks by the Midianites, he was called by the angel of the Lord to save his people. After asking God for a sign the order had really come from him, Gideon sent out a call to arms, to which 32,000 men responded. God reckoned these were too many and told Gideon to send away all those who were not too happy about fighting. Gideon obeyed and was left with 10,000 men. This number also God thought was too great and he ordered Gideon to test them further. Eventually Gideon was left with 300 men under his command, 300 proper soldiers. In a precursor to the David and Goliath story, Gideon and his tiny troop emerge victorious from the ensuing battle.

Samson

Samson, a member of the tribe of Dan, consecrated at birth as a Nazarite, that is, someone dedicated to the service of God, was a heroic figure about whom are told stories featuring great exploits of strength and courage. The parents of Samson, like those of several other Biblical heroes, had despaired of ever having a child, and promised, if they were given a son, to dedicate him to the service of the Lord. The conditions that went along with the gift were that Samson must never eat grapes, drink wine or vinegar, or let a razor near his hair. By obeying these restrictions, Samson grew to possess superhuman strength, wrestling and killing a lion among other exploits.

It was during Samson's life that the Philistine threat arose against the Hebrew people. Settling along the coast, the Philistines posed a real danger to the Israelites, especially the more remote tribes of Dan and Judah. Having been handed over to his enemies by men of Judah, Samson broke his bonds and escaped, after first slaying a thousand Philistines with the jawbone of an ass. After many other adventures and a short-lived marriage to a Philistine woman, Samson fell in love with another woman, probably also a Philistine, who betrayed him when he told her the secret of his great strength - his hair, which had never been cut. This woman, Delilah, cut off his hair, his strength vanished, he was taken prisoner and blinded by the Philistines. They, however, gradually became careless, not noticing that his hair had grown long once more, and brought him into their temple where a great assembly of 3000 men and women had gathered to honour the pagan god Dagon. Praying to God to give him strength, Samson seized two pillars with such force that they shattered and the temple collapsed on all those assembled, including Samson himself. The Scriptures record that he slew even more Philistines in death than he ever did in life.

Samson and the other heroes are powerful witnesses to the saving power of God, who remained with his people and called some to act in the defence of the others. Through his will, God gave such heroes the strength and will to act, for "nothing is impossible to God" (*Lk* 1:37). "They are the ones he chose specially long ago and intended to become true images of his Son, so that his Son might be the eldest of many brothers. He called those he intended for this; those he called he justified, and with those he justified he shared his glory" (*Rm* 8:30).

The Kings: David and Solomon

God speaks, Israel listens

God continued to communicate with his people through specially chosen servants. One of the best-known of these was Samuel, singled out for service to God from his early childhood. His parents, like Samson's before him (and like the parents of John the Baptist centuries later), were childless for many years. His mother, Hannah, promised that if God would only give her a child she would pledge him to God's service from infancy. Thus, Samuel grew up in the household of the high priest Eli in Shiloh, at that time where the Ark of the Covenant was kept. There is a delightful story of how Samuel became aware of his calling. One night a voice awoke the boy, calling his name. Assuming it was Eli needing him, he immediately ran to the priest. After this had happened for the third time, Eli realised that God had been calling the boy and he sent him back to his bed, telling him to respond next time the voice called him, saying: "Speak, Lord, your servant is listening" (*1 S* 4:9).

The Hebrew people were a small nation surrounded by more powerful peoples and had to be constantly on their guard. While Samuel was still a boy, war broke out between Israel and the Philistines. The Israelites asked for the Ark of the Covenant to be sent from Shiloh, believing that thus the Lord would necessarily be with them and could save them from their enemies. The Philistines, however, slaughtered thousands of the Hebrew army and seized the Ark, carrying it off to their city of Ashdod, by the Mediterranean Sea, halfway between Gaza and Joppa. There they placed it in the temple of their god Dagon, right next to the idol of their god. Strange things began to happen in the temple: the statue of the pagan god was knocked over and damaged, then plagues broke out amongst the people, so the Philistines became afraid and moved the Ark. In the other cities where they took it, however, the same thing happened. Eventually, in fear, they placed the Ark in a chariot pulled by cows which were left to go where they pleased. The cows went to the land of the Israelites and the Ark was safely returned. This shows that although we cannot compel God to help us, nevertheless he does not abandon his people even in their sins.

The people demand a king

The Hebrews became jealous of their neighbours who had kings to rule over them and so they persisted in demanding that they also be given a king. Samuel, who by this time had grown up and become a prophet as well as a priest, relayed their demands to God. Through Samuel, God warned the Israelites of the dangers of having a king, but they insisted. One danger was that the Israelites would come to trust in a strong king, rather than in the protecting power of God, the true King of Israel: we, too, can easily rely on human strength rather than on God's care for us.

Saul, of the tribe of Benjamin, was chosen to be the first king of Israel. He had already proved himself to be an able battle commander and seemed the right choice, though he was not universally popular with the people. He later proved to be less than effective, however, often ignoring Samuel's advice and usurping his position as priest. Eventually the Israelites ended up facing real danger at the hands of the Philistines who had a particularly mighty warrior, the giant Goliath.

This brings us to the next really important person in God's plan of salvation for humankind: King David. Samuel had already pronounced that none of Saul's sons would be king after him and now God sent Samuel to anoint Saul's successor as king. Anointing was a sure sign of God's favour, used only for kings and high priests. The person God chose to be the next king turned out to be the youngest son of a man named Jesse from Bethlehem in Judaea: a mere youth who tended his father's sheep. But God does not see as men see and he insisted that David was his choice. Overthrowing all expectations, the boy David slew Goliath, was hailed as a great hero by the people of Israel and became a favourite of Saul and his son Jonathan. David was also an accomplished musician and he was invited to stay at court in order to cheer the king with his music.

David also became a very successful warrior, so successful indeed that Saul grew jealous of him and sought to kill him. David fled into the wilderness where he gathered around him a band of outlawed warriors. His great friend Jonathan, Saul's son, tried to reconcile his father and David, but to no avail. Taking advantage of the situation, the Philistines once again attacked Israel, and Saul bravely led his army against them. Many of the Israelites were slain, including Jonathan and his brothers. In grief and despair, Saul fell upon his sword and died. David, overcome with grief when he heard the tragic news, lamented: "Alas, the glory of Israel has been slain on your heights! How did the heroes fall?" (2 S 1:19)

Thus, eventually David became king. He too sinned and fell from grace, by appropriating Bathsheba, another man's wife, and arranging her husband's death. He was called to repentance by the prophet Nathan and God forgave him, though there were far-reaching consequences, one of which was that David was not considered worthy to build the Temple. David continued to perform feats of courage and is also credited with composing many of the Psalms, the Hebrew prayer book. The city of Jerusalem which had been occupied by the Jebusite people was recaptured by David, thus securing his power as king of all Israel. To show to all people the sacred nature of his new capital city, David ordered the Ark of the Covenant to be brought into Jerusalem. Scripture gives us a beautiful description of how David danced for joy as the Ark of the Covenant was finally carried into the city.

Success and disobedience

Solomon, a son of David and Bathsheba, became king after him and was renowned for his wisdom, the gift he had asked of God. He built the great Temple in Jerusalem, a work that took seven years and was carried out by around 200,000 labourers under 3300 foremen and supervisors. Vast quantities of cedar and cypress wood were shipped from Tyre in Phoenicia, along with skilled craftsmen, including the bronzesmith Hiram, reckoned by some to be the architect of the Temple. However, Solomon too fell into sinful living. Taking many foreign wives and concubines, he was led by them into sacrificing to pagan gods. Because of this, God foretold that his kingdom would be split in two after his death. Solomon saw worldly glory and success, which were gifts from God, as coming from his own efforts, and thus became careless of God's primacy.

After King Solomon's death, the kingdom was indeed torn apart. The tribes of Judah and Benjamin remained loyal to Solomon's son, King Rehoboam, in the southern kingdom known as Judah, with Jerusalem its capital. The northern kingdom, comprising the other ten tribes, became known as Israel, under King Jeroboam. This happened around 975 BC and war carried on between the two kingdoms for sixty years before an alliance was formed. Rather confusingly, at times we find the whole Hebrew people referred to as "Israel" or the "sons of Israel", "Israel" also being the name given to Jacob. (Israel did not become the definitive name for the whole Hebrew people until after the Exile in Babylon.) Jeroboam introduced "calf worship" to Israel, ordering the people to go no longer up to Jerusalem to worship. This policy was followed by his successors and so the people were led deeper into sin. God then called a succession of prophets to persuade his people to come back to him.

The Prophets: Elijah and Elisha

Wishing to save his people from the consequences of their wilful disobedience, God called a series of prophets to warn the people to turn their hearts back to him. In the Old Testament a prophet was not someone who predicted the future but rather one who communicated divine revelation. A prophet was often chosen by God to demonstrate to the people, and to their enemies, the power of one true God. An older title for prophet was "seer", the description given, for instance, to Samuel. The prophets were, to a greater or lesser extent, an extremely significant group and their "books" make up the largest section of the Old Testament; many of these figures are also mentioned in the history books. The Hebrew people of Jesus's time would have known the stories of the prophets and would have been on the lookout for any "signs" from their prophecies, especially those associated with the coming of God's Messiah.

Elijah

The prophet most mentioned in the New Testament is Elijah, who made his first appearance in 1 Kings 17 when he was sent to Ahab, the seventh king of Israel. Ahab had come under the evil influence of his wicked wife Jezebel and, to the calf worship introduced by Jeroboam, he added worship of Baal, a false god worshipped by many eastern peoples. Elijah was sent by God to bring the people of Israel back to the righteous path and to prove that the God of their ancestors, of Abraham, Isaac and Jacob, was the one true God and therefore infinitely more powerful than the Baals worshipped by the pagans. Elijah warned Ahab that his impiety would be punished by prolonged drought and famine.

Immediately after this, God told Elijah to flee into the desert to prepare for future confrontations. In the desert, ravens brought him bread and meat each day. Later God ordered him to leave the desert and lodge with a widow at Zarephath, a place lying between the ancient cities of Tyre and Sidon, where God worked a miracle through Elijah. Despite having only enough food for one final meal for herself and her son, before facing death, the widow of Zarephath fed her guest and from then on she was destined never to run out of flour and oil. Later, when her son fell ill and died, Elijah prayed to God over the body and the boy was restored to life, foreshadowing the resurrections performed by Jesus.

Hoping to end the drought devastating his lands, Ahab agreed to meet Elijah on Mount Carmel where it was proposed that sacrifices should be publicly offered, for the purpose of determining whether Baal or the God of Israel was in fact the true God. After a dramatic confrontation, with taunts from both sides, Elijah's God was seen to be victorious and the people fell on their faces, crying, "The Lord is God." Thus was accomplished the great work of Elijah's ministry. The prophets of Baal were then put to death by Elijah. There immediately followed rain, according to his word, and in answer to his prayers.

The enraged Jezebel threatened to put Elijah to death and he fled into the wilderness, sinking into a sleep of depression. An angel awoke him, giving him food and water and telling him to journey to Mount Horeb. Obedient as always, Elijah travelled for forty days and forty nights to Horeb, the mountain of the Lord, where he waited in a cave for further instructions. The Lord appeared to him and spoke to him, not in a mighty wind, or earthquake, or fire, but in "a gentle breeze": "What are you doing here, Elijah?" (*1 K* 18:39; 19:13) Elijah offers us a salutary lesson in prayer, in communicating with God, "for thus says the Lord...your salvation lay in conversion and tranquillity, your strength, in complete trust" (*Is* 30:15); and, as Jesus himself was to teach, we hear God, not in a babble of noise, but in the silence of our hearts: "But when you pray, go to your private room and, when you have shut your door, pray to your Father who is in that secret place, and your Father who sees all that is done in secret will reward you" (*Mt* 6:6). To strengthen Elijah in his despair at feeling he had failed his Lord, God manifested to him the divine glory, then gave him further instructions, telling him to appoint Elisha as his successor.

Incidentally, Ahab repented and was reprieved by God although his royal line came to an end after he died fighting against the Aramaeans when his son Ahaziah "did what is displeasing to the Lord, by following the example of his father and mother" (*1 K* 22:53). Jezebel came to a very nasty end, being thrown out of a window, trampled on by horses and devoured by dogs, just as had been foretold by God through his prophet.

Elijah was finally rewarded for his faithful service to God by being carried straight up to heaven in a fiery chariot. The Jewish people to this day believe that he will return as forerunner to the Messiah and they continue to set a place for him at their Passover supper. In the New Testament we read in all three Synoptic Gospels how Elijah appeared with Moses when Jesus was transfigured on Mount Tabor, in the presence of Peter, John and James. While Moses signified the Law, Elijah represented the prophets, and both were believed to have been taken straight up into heaven as a reward for their service.

Elisha

All that remained on earth of Elijah was his cloak, symbolic of his prophetic ministry, which he gave to his successor, Elisha. It is from this incident that we derive the expression "inheriting the mantle" or "wearing the mantle", in connection with the successors of great people.

Elisha also inherited his predecessor's gift of miracles. He performed two for the wife of a wealthy landowner of Shunem: first promising her a son despite her husband's great age and later calling the child back to life when he died. Another miracle associated with Elisha was one well-known to the people in Jesus' time: Naaman, an Aramaean general, contracted leprosy but was told by a little Israelite slave girl that "the prophet of Samaria" could cure him. Elisha told him to "go and bathe seven times in the Jordan, and your flesh will become clean once more". Naaman was at first rather annoyed that this so-called prophet had not even invoked God or laid hands on him, but was persuaded by his servants to do as Elisha said; "and his flesh became clean once more like the flesh of a little child" (2 K 5:3,10,14). Elisha performed many other wonders, including a "multiplication of loaves" prefiguring Jesus's miracle of the loaves and fishes (2 K 4:42-44). Where Elijah became renowned as one of the truly great religious personalities of Israel, Elisha was admired as a worker of wonders and for his political acumen and influence. He is mentioned, as is Elijah, by Jesus, according to St Luke. Both prophets operated during a time of great devastation and suffering: "There were many widows in Israel, I can assure you, in Elijah's day, when...famine raged throughout the land, but Elijah was not sent to any one of these: he was sent to a widow at Zarephath, a Sidonian town. And in the prophet Elisha's time there were many lepers in Israel, but none of these was cured, except the Syrian, Naaman" (*Lk* 4:25-27). When his own time came, Jesus ignored no one who appealed to him for healing but, when he saw their faith, cured them and sent them away whole.

There were many other men chosen by God to bear his word to his people. They tend to be divided into "greater" or lesser" prophets but all performed a significant part in God's plan of salvation as it gradually unfolded throughout the generations. The prophets became especially important during the time of the exile.

The Great Prophets: Isaiah, Jeremiah, Ezekiel and Daniel

God chose from amongst his people many prophets to warn them of the terrible consequences of turning away from him and following the evil ways of their pagan neighbours and captors. Out of his great love for the people he had chosen, he longed for them to return to him and, through the prophets, he told them also of the graces to come for those who were faithful.

Isaiah - God promises his coming kingdom

Of the four "great" Prophets, Isaiah is the one from whom we hear most during Advent and Lent. Born around 765 BC in the kingdom of Judah, he exercised his prophetic ministry for around forty years, which saw the growing threat to Israel and Judah from Assyria. Not all prophets were as clear about their call from God as was Isaiah, although he was convinced of his unworthiness for the task:

"What a wretched state I am in! I am lost, for I am a man of unclean lips"…Then one of the seraphs flew to me, holding in his hand a live coal which he had taken from the altar with a pair of tongs. With this he touched my mouth (*Is* 6:5-6).

If one's lips are touched by divine fire one becomes an eloquent carrier of God's word. Isaiah's mission was to proclaim the fall of Israel and Judah as punishment for the people's infidelity to the Covenant. The book that bears his name collects various other prophecies written at different times; amongst these are several about the promised Messiah, God's servant who would save his people. It is this part of the book of Isaiah that gives us the three "Songs of the Suffering Servant" which we associate with Jesus and hear during Holy Week.

And yet ours were the sufferings he bore,
ours the sorrows he carried.
But we, we thought of him as someone punished,
struck by God, and brought low.
Yet he was pierced through for our faults,
crushed for our sins.
On him lies a punishment that brings us peace,
and through his wounds we are healed (*Is* 53:4-5).

The Messiah was to bring about a new paradise where all creation would once more live in harmony. As well as warnings, the writings associated with Isaiah offer hope of eternal life and a beautiful vision of original harmony restored, a kingdom paradise of peace and love.

> The wolf lives with the lamb,
> the panther lies down with the kid,
> calf and lion cub feed together
> with a little boy to lead them (*Is* 11:6).

Jeremiah - God prepares his people for suffering

Jeremiah was called by God as a prophet while a young man in 628 BC, leaving his home and going to live in Jerusalem where he assisted King Josiah in his work of reformation. During the reign of King Jehoiakim he fell into disfavour; prophets were often disliked and feared as their prophecies made people uncomfortable. Jehoiakim asked Jeremiah to write down his predictions and then, in a rage, destroyed the scroll on which they were written. Jeremiah remained in Jerusalem, uttering warnings about the city's inevitable fall, but was ignored. He was still there when Nebuchadnezzar besieged the city in 589 BC. Some of the most poignant, yet beautiful, words in Scripture are attributed to Jeremiah lamenting over the destruction of Jerusalem. In some monasteries at the Office of Vigils on Good Friday and Holy Saturday, in place of the usual readings, passages from Lamentations are chanted. In these readings the pain of all suffering humanity is contained in heart-breaking beauty, suffering which would be redeemed through Christ's saving death and resurrection.

> All you who pass this way,
> look and see:
> is any sorrow like the sorrow
> that afflicts me,
> with which the Lord has struck me
> on the day of his burning anger? (*Lm* 1:12)

The Exile

In 606 BC Nebuchadnezzar, the most powerful of all the Babylonian kings, invaded Judah (*Jr* 25:1) and carried away some royal youths, together with the sacred vessels of the temple (*2 Ch* 36:7; *Dn* 1:2). In 598 BC (*Jr* 52:28; *2 K* 24:12), he carried away captive 3000 eminent Jews, including the king (*2 Ch* 36:10), his family and officers, a large number of warriors, and very many important persons and artisans (*2 K* 24:12-16), leaving behind only the poor and helpless. This was the first general deportation to Babylon. Then, in 588 BC, after the revolt of King Zedekiah, there was a second general deportation of Jews by Nebuchadnezzar (*Jr* 52:29; *2 K* 25:8), including eight hundred more of the most important men. He carried away also the rest of the sacred vessels (*2 Ch* 36:18). This time, from the destruction of the Temple (*2*

K 25:9) to its restoration in 517 BC under King Cyrus of Persia (*Ez* 1-6), is the period of the "seventy years" of the Exile. Finally, in 582 BC, came the last deportation when 4600 heads of families were carried off with their wives and children and dependants (*Jr* 52:30; 43:5-7; *2 Ch* 36:20, etc.). Thus the exiles came to form a considerable community in Babylon. When Cyrus granted permission to the Jews to return to their own land (*Ez* 1:5; 7:13), only a comparatively small number at first took the opportunity, though eventually many belonging to the kingdom of Israel returned to Jerusalem (*Jr* 50:4,5,17-20,33-35). Many, however, decided to settle in the land of Babylon. This event of Exile was for many Israelites utterly baffling: how could it be reconciled with God's promises to Abraham, Moses and King David? If God's word could not be trusted, did anything make sense any more? To answer these questions, which are our questions too whenever we meet an event that casts doubt on God's love for us, God sent further prophets.

Ezekiel - new life even amidst death

When the sinner renounces sin to become law-abiding and honest, he deserves to live (*Ezk* 18:27).

Ezekiel (the name means "God will strengthen") was one of the Jewish exiles who settled at Tel-Abib, on the banks of the Kebar, "in the land of the Chaldeans". He was probably carried away captive with Jehoiachin (*Ezk* 1:2; *2 K* 24:14-16) around 597 BC, ten years before the fall of Jerusalem. His prophetic call came to him "in the fifth year of exile for King Jehoiachin" (594 BC). He had a house in the place of his exile, where he lost his wife, in the ninth year of his exile (*Ezk* 8:1; 24:18). Ezekiel held a prominent place among the exiles, and was often consulted by the elders (*Ezk* 8:1; 11:25; 14:1; 20:1). His ministry lasted for twenty-three years (595-573 BC), during part of which he was contemporaneous with Jeremiah. The date and manner of his death are unknown. His tomb is reputed to be near Baghdad, at a place called Keffil.

Ezekiel denounced the unfaithfulness of the people (*Ezk* 3:22-24), warning them - in contrast to the words of false prophets (*Ezk* 4:1-3) - of the certain destruction of Jerusalem. He had several visions, some of which are referred to in the Book of Revelation. In one vision he saw a field covered with bones which, through the Lord, he resurrected and transformed into a mighty army: "He said, 'Prophesy over these bones. Say, "Dry bones, hear the word of the Lord"'" (*Ezk* 37:4). Another vision is of God on a fiery throne surrounded by four winged creatures with the faces of a man, an eagle, an ox and a lion (these are also mentioned in the Book of Revelation and became associated with the four Evangelists). Much of the symbolism in Ezekiel has been associated with the sacraments, especially with baptism, and the last Old Testament reading at the Easter Vigil is a passage from Ezekiel pointing towards baptism: "for the sake of my holy name...I shall pour clean water over you and you will be cleansed...I shall give you a new heart, and put a new spirit in you" (*Ezk* 36:22, 25-26).

Ezekiel also made prophecies against surrounding nations: the Ammonites, Moabites, Edomites, Philistines, the cities of Tyre and Sidon, and against Egypt. He made yet more prophecies after the destruction of Jerusalem by Nebuchadnezzar: about the triumphs of Israel and of the kingdom of God on earth, the Messianic times, and the establishment and prosperity of the kingdom of God. In all of this, we should not be distracted by the sometimes confusing historical background; what Ezekiel conveys is a renewed promise from God, one not based in an earthly kingdom like Solomon's but in God's reign through the making new of the human heart, filling it with his love and mercy.

Daniel

The book of Daniel purports to be written by an educated young man from a noble family, deported into Babylon where he became a servant at Nebuchadnezzar's court. He could interpret dreams and proved a capable administrator, but he remained faithful to Jewish law and practices, thereby making many enemies. When

Nebuchadnezzar's son Belshazzar succeeded him as king, he held a magnificent banquet for all his court, using the silver and gold sacred vessels his father plundered from the Temple in Jerusalem. Suddenly a mysterious hand appeared and wrote letters on the wall that none of the king's wise men were able to read or understand. The frightened king sent for Daniel who read the words *Mene*, *Tekel*, *Parsin*, meaning "measured, weighed, divided", and explained their meaning: "*Mene*: God has measured your sovereignty and put an end to it; *Tekel*: you have been weighed in the balance and found wanting; *Parsin*: your kingdom has been divided and given to the Medes and the Persians." That night Belshazzar was killed and Darius the Persian seized his kingdom (*Dn* 5:26-31).

Darius took a liking to Daniel and appointed him one of his three top officials. Jealous of Daniel, the other advisers got Darius to approve a decree which forbade anyone to pray to any god or man who was not the king, under pain of being thrown into a den of lions. Daniel continued to be faithful to Jewish law and worshipped only the one true God and Darius reluctantly had him thrown into the lions' den, while saying to him: "Your God himself, whom you have served so faithfully, will have to save you." The lions, although starving, ignored Daniel and when Darius found him safe Daniel told him that his God had sent an angel to help him. It is not clear which historical Persian king Darius represents; the historical King Darius ruled later than Cyrus, the King of Persia who finally allowed the Jews to return home and rebuild the Temple in Jerusalem, so the Book of Daniel should be seen as a story rather than a work of history, but a story that illustrates the strength of faith and trust in God, and that worship should be given to God alone, however many pressures may surround us to do otherwise. As St Peter warns us: "Be calm but vigilant, because your enemy the devil is prowling round like a roaring lion, looking for someone to eat. Stand up to him, strong in faith and in the knowledge that your brothers all over the world are suffering the same things" (*1 P* 5:8-9).

God's many messengers

There are numerous other prophets in the history of Israel, many of whom have books attributed to them. For example, Baruch, whom we hear read at the Easter Vigil, was companion and scribe to Jeremiah. Their task was always either to warn the people of the consequences of turning away from the Lord or to relay to them God's promises of redemption. Prophets were often feared, hated and attacked, and tended to be solitary. It was not an easy job. As Jesus sadly remarked many years later, a prophet is seldom listened to in his own country. The history books and the books of the prophets often contain the same or similar stories, told from a different perspective.

Lastly, the Books of the Maccabees recount the heroic struggles between the Jews and their Syrian enemies in the forty years until 134 BC. The Jewish people were led by Judas Maccabeus and his two brothers. These books have a strongly religious purpose and a climax was reached with a description of the rededication of the Temple. The Second Book of Maccabees gives us several references to particular doctrines pointing towards Catholic teaching: the resurrection of the body; rewards and punishments after death; prayers for the dead; and the intercession of the saints. "For if he had not expected the fallen to rise again it would have been superfluous and foolish to pray for the dead, whereas if he had in mind the splendid recompense reserved for those who make a pious end, the thought was holy and devout. This was why he had this atonement sacrifice offered for the dead, so that they might be released from their sin" (*2 M* 12:44-5).

Then, in the New Testament, we encounter "the last of the prophets": John the Baptist. His father prophesied at his birth that John would be "called prophet of the Most High": his was the "voice crying in the wilderness: 'prepare a way for the Lord'" (*Mt* 3:3). He preached a baptism of repentance in preparation for the kingdom of God and gathered many disciples around him. One day, coming towards him, he saw Jesus whom he recognised as the awaited Messiah. "Behold the Lamb of God, who takes away the sin of the world," he told his disciples (*Jn* 1:29). Jesus, the sinless Son of God, stood among sinful men and asked John to baptise him. Thus began Jesus Christ's ministry on earth and the culmination of God's plan of salvation for humankind.

In the Fullness of Time

At various times in the past and in various different ways, God spoke to our ancestors through the prophets; but in our own time, the last days, he has spoken to us through his Son, the Son that he has appointed to inherit everything and through whom he made everything there is (*Heb* 1:2).

We have arrived at the final stage of God's eternal plan of salvation for his children. Our ancestors lived through the age of the Father and the first coming of the Son; we are now living in the age of the Spirit and the Church, the "last days", but we must always remember with patience and obedience that to God "'a day' can mean a thousand years, *and a thousand years is like a day*" (*2 P* 3:8, quoting *Ps* 90:4); and only the Father "knows the hour" (*Mt* 24:36) of the consummation of the world. "In Jesus", says the Catechism, "God recapitulates all of his history of salvation on behalf of men" (*CCC* 430).

In Luke's Gospel we encounter Zechariah, a priest of the Old Covenant, father of the last of the prophets, John the Baptist. At first struck dumb for his lack of trust in God's promises, Zechariah's voice is restored at the birth of his son and he gives tongue to the canticle the Church proclaims each day at Morning Prayer, the *Benedictus*, that exultant prayer of thanksgiving for God's saving interventions throughout history: "Blessed be the Lord God of Israel, for he has visited and redeemed his people" (*Lk* 1:68ff).

A New Covenant

> This cup is the new covenant in my blood which will be poured out for you (*Lk* 22:20).

Through his Son, his Word become flesh, the fulfilment of all his promises, God offered a New Covenant to all people, written not on stone or parchment but in the Person of that Son and transcribed by him on the hearts of those who accepted him. In that Covenant, Jesus is the "Way, and the Truth, and the Life" (*Jn* 14:6). He is the Truth because it is through his teaching, which comes from the Father, that we learn what we must know in order to reach our heavenly destination. This teaching he bequeathed to his Church, to guard, interpret and hand on to future generations. He is also the Way, since through his example he showed us how to live in this world, in order to attain eternal life in the next: to accept God's Commandments into our hearts and to live according to the Beatitudes. He is our Life, because he gave as gifts to his bride the Church, the Eucharist and the other sacraments, which continue to nourish us and to heal us in every part of our lives. He even gave us his own prayer, the Our Father.

> If your lips confess that Jesus is Lord and if you believe in your heart that God raised him from the dead, then you will be saved (*Rm* 10:9).

It is easy to imagine that we are automatically "saved" and infallibly certain of heaven merely because we have at one single moment of our lives accepted Jesus as our Redeemer. We can be certain that God desires each one of us to make our home with him at the last, and that Christ died on the Cross for each one of us; but, for Paul, being "saved" means a profession of faith which we continue to confess and live out in our lives: a daily dying and rising with Christ, a continual conversion of life, constantly turning back to God in prayer and repentance.

The Church makes God's Covenant present

It has been said that God created the world for the sake of the Church, a Church through which is mediated the New Covenant sealed in the precious Blood of Christ his Son. That Son did not "leave [us] orphans" but passed on to us the Holy Spirit, the Counsellor, to "teach [us] everything and remind you of" everything that Jesus taught, "starting with Moses and going through all the prophets...the passages throughout the scriptures that were about himself" (*Jn* 14:18, 26; *Lk* 24:27). "Christ is Lord of the cosmos and of history. In him human history and indeed all creation are 'set forth' and transcendently fulfilled" (*CCC* 668).

The *Catechism* reminds us how "the liturgical celebration always refers to God's saving interventions in history" and "'makes a remembrance' of the marvellous works of God" (*CCC* 1103) and so in every Mass, through the readings and in the Eucharistic Prayers, we call to mind, over and over, how God has loved and guided his children throughout the long centuries of our existence.

> But when the appointed time came, God sent his Son, born of a woman, born a subject of the Law, to redeem the subjects of the Law and to enable us to be adopted as sons. The proof that you are sons is that God has sent the Spirit of his Son into our hearts: the Spirit that cries, 'Abba, Father!' (*Ga* 4:4-6).

Those of us now living in these last days have had many blessings poured out upon us: through the New Covenant we can acknowledge God as our Father, Jesus as our Saviour and brother and the Holy Spirit as our advocate and comforter. We have the immaculate Mother of God as our intercessor and model of faith in God's promises; and we can look to the example of the saints who have gone ahead, "on whose constant intercession in [God's] presence we rely for unfailing help" (Eucharistic Prayer

III). Through the sacraments we encounter the crucified, risen and glorified Lord and enter anew into the New Covenant, each time rising with rekindled strength into that new life in Christ. Each time Christ gives himself freely to us in the Eucharist we should rejoice:

> "Take this, all of you!" What a mystery! Jesus has united me to himself in the most sublime and holiest act in history; in the only act really "worthy of God", worthy of His holiness and His majesty. Let the heavens marvel, the earth exult, the angels rejoice, the demons tremble: God has obtained what the universe was created for; His plan and wish have been fulfilled; nothing could prevent it, not even sin; His creature went back to Him in a spontaneous gesture of love; he has given in sacrifice what he has received from God as a gift (Raniero Cantalamessa, *The Eucharist*, Liturgical Press, 1995).

Keep running steadily in the race we have started. Let us not lose sight of Jesus, who leads us in our faith and brings it to perfection: for the sake of the joy which was still in the future, he endured the cross, disregarding the shamefulness of it, and from now on has taken his place at the right of God's throne (*Heb* 12:1-2).

CTS New Catholic Bible - Paperback

The only Bible with the translations approved for use in the Lectionary. Jerusalem Bible translation with Grail Psalms.

- Especially commissioned introductions, one for each book, giving the biblical and historical context
- Especially commissioned liturgical introductions placing each book of the Bible in the Church's liturgical year
- New footnotes following the latest scholarship
- New marginal references helping you get the most out of each passage
- New layout – using clear and modern fonts in easy-to-read single-column format
- New text alterations, replacing the 'Tetragrammaton' (name of God) with 'the Lord' as requested by Pope Benedict XVI for all new Bibles
- New directories of references for readings used in the Mass and the Liturgy of the Hours, including the fuller two-year cycle for the Breviary

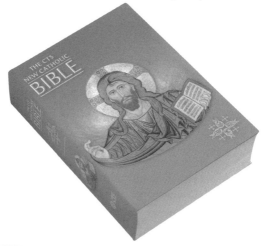

Sc108 ISBN 978 1 86082 831 7